AF143880

BOOK ANALYSIS

By Jessica Wheeler

A Modest Proposal

BY JONATHAN SWIFT

Bright
≡Summaries.com

JONATHAN SWIFT

IRISH WRITER OF FICTION AND NON-FICTION

- **Born in Dublin in 1667.**
- **Died in Dublin in 1745.**
- **Notable works:**
  - *A Tale of a Tub* (1704), novel
  - *Gulliver's Travels* (1726), novel
  - *Directions to Servants* (1745), essay

Jonathan Swift was born in Dublin in 1667 to English-born parents Jonathan and Abigail Swift. He was their second child. His father had travelled to Ireland with his brother when their family estate in England was lost, and both brothers sought to make their fortunes in the practice of law. Swift's father died a few months before his birth, leaving his mother to seek the help of relatives in order to survive with her young son and daughter.

Swift attended Kilkenny College until the age of 15, and received an undergraduate degree from

Trinity College in Dublin. He moved to England in 1688 and took up a secretarial position with Sir William Temple, a British diplomat. Swift resided in Moor Park, Farnham, which was the home of Sir William Temple, until his employer's sudden death in 1699. During this time he began writing poetry.

Swift is best known for his wit and political satires, but he wrote much throughout his career and was recognised by many of his literary peers as a great author.

A MODEST PROPOSAL

- **Genre:** satirical essay
- **Reference edition:** Swift, J. (1996) *A Modest Proposal and Other Satirical Works*. New York: Dover Publications Inc.
- **1st edition:** 1729
- **Themes:** Irish society, poverty, class, power, the abuse of power, suffering, morality, politics,

The full title of this text is *A Modest Proposal: for preventing the children of poor people in Ireland from being a burthen to their parents or country, and for making them beneficial to the public,* but it is commonly known by the shortened title of *A Modest Proposal.* Swift wrote this essay and published in anonymously in 1729. This text is a satirical commentary on 18th-century Irish society and its treatment of the lower classes.

Swift uses this satirical style to deliver a shocking political message. He spends the first part of the essay lamenting the sufferings of the Irish people, and follows this up by arguing with the support of detached logic and reason that the only solution is to fatten the young Irish children up and sell them to the wealthy upper classes as a delicacy. Of course, the purpose of this outrageous suggestion is to seize the attention of the masses and provoke thought and accountability for the state of Irish society at the time.

SUMMARY

Swift opens his essay by calling the sight of poor Irish beggars "a melancholy object" (p. 52). He describes "beggars of the female sex, followed by three, four or six children, all in rags and importuning every passenger for an alms" (*ibid.*) and draws attention to the fact that these mothers cannot work when they have their young children to care for. Swift contends that these conditions of poverty continue through the generations and lead the infants that belong to these poor mothers into equally dire conditions in adulthood.

According to Swift, this "prodigious number of children" (*ibid.*) are an "additional grievance" (*ibid.*) to the Irish society of his time, which was already in a "deplorable state" (*ibid.*). He says, therefore, that the answer for the improvement of conditions must be found in a solution that deals with this large number of young dependents, who require nourishment from society but cannot give back anything of value in return due to their infancy. Swift claims that the resolution he will propose will apply to all children over the age of one year whose parents are not adequately equipped to support them, but he does not only mean the children of beggars.

Swift outlines his calculations, which estimate that there are 120 000 children born each year of Irish parents who cannot afford to raise them. He goes on to detail his proposed solution for these thousands of children.

Swift states that he has been informed by an American acquaintance that "a young healthy child well nursed is at a year old a most delicious, nourishing, and wholesome food" (p. 53), and therefore "humbly offer[s] it to public consideration" (p. 54) that 20 000 of the 120 000 children he has calculated be kept for breeding purposes. A quarter of this 20 000 should be males, which Swift says is similar to the allowance made for breeding of sheep and cattle. Swift contends that the other 100 000 should be sold as food "to the persons of quality and fortune throughout the kingdom" (*ibid.*).

Swift calculates the cost of nursing a child to the age of one year and the price the child could be sold for and concludes that the profit the mother would make on each child would be eight shillings, and she would then be fit to work until she bears another child. Swift says that a friend of his made a comment on this plan and suggested that the many children between the ages of 12 and 14 who are starving throughout the country for want of work be sold in the same way as these infants to supplement the demand for venison. However, he disagrees with this suggestion as the flesh of teenage boys especially is reported to be tough and of a disagreeable taste. Furthermore, Swift says, this would be bordering on cruelty and therefore objectionable to him on these grounds.

Swift acknowledges that the sick and disabled are another burden on Ireland's struggling economy at the time of writing his essay, but he quickly dismisses the urgency of finding a solution for this group as they are dying off quickly anyway. He goes on from this point to list a number of advantages for the strategy that he has suggested, which then leads him to admit that there may be one objection to his plan – the reduction of the population. Swift counters this potential criticism by saying that reducing the population is in fact one of the goals of his plan, and it is necessary in Ireland, which is the only state he intends the approach to be implemented in.

Swift concludes the essay by outlining some of the solutions that have been suggested by others before him and expounding on how they have not been adequate to resolve Ireland's difficulties. He says that, despite this, he is not so sure of his own opinion that he would dismiss that of other "wise men". Nevertheless, he insists that these alternatives effectively deal with the primary issues of the "100,000 useless mouths and backs" (p. 58) which must be fed and provided for, and the harsh sufferings of the countless Irish men and women who may well profess that they would rather have been sold as food at the age of one year than have lived to shoulder the hardships they do.

CONTEXT

At the time of writing this essay, Ireland had been under British rule for a number of centuries. A Protestant aristocracy was well established, and the country was controlled by English landlords and politicians. Landlords charged high rents to their Irish tenants, who struggled to pay and keep a roof over their heads. Trade laws and high taxes made it impossible for the Irish economy to prosper, whilst the rights of Irish citizens to take part in politics or pursue an education were also impeded by British laws. The Irish people were not only oppressed by British rule, but secured in this subjugation so effectively that they had no possible way of fighting back. Poverty and starvation became a standard part of Irish life, and these hardships often resulted in death. In effect, the tyrannical British rule was responsible for killing many Irish men and women. Some tried to flee, often to America, but as the lowest of classes, the conditions they faced on the long journey were often just as difficult to survive as life in Ireland was.

Although Swift was of English descent, and a member of the wealthy and powerful Anglo-Irish class, he sympathised with the poverty-stricken Irish population and was disgusted by the treatment they received from the British. Swift became more involved in politics from the turn of the 18th century, and expressed his political opinions through pamphleteering. *A Modest Proposal* was originally published in pamphlet form. Pamphleteers used this form to bring about change or incite members of society to debate on the political and economic issues they chose to write about. Swift's essay targets the British aristocracy, who largely ignored the message and saw the text purely as a piece of entertainment.

ANALYSIS

SATIRE

A Modest Proposal is a Juvenalian satire, which means it is a more scathing type of satirical style. It is so named after the Roman poet Juvenal (late 1st and early 2nd century CE), who was author of the collection of satirical poems entitled *The Satires* (early 2nd century CE). Satire is a commonly used literary device which is often employed for the purpose of social criticism. A key feature of all satirical writing is an openly sarcastic tone. Other trademarks of this style are irony, exaggeration and far-fetched comparisons; this can be seen in Swift's text when he compares Irish infants sold as food for the rich landlord's table to other kinds of meat reared for consumption.

Satirical writing draws direct attention to social issues without the expectation of providing a solution. Political satire often falls into the Juvenalian category as it is more cutting and less likely to contain humour. Juvenalian satire is often more shocking to the reader, a feature which is intentional. This abrasive quality is implemented purposely to secure a more impassioned reaction from readers. In this essay, Swift juxtaposes a shockingly unethical proposal with a series of supremely logical but morally detached supporting arguments in order to draw attention to the attitude in which other solutions have been proposed before him. Through his comparison of Irish children to mere animals who are reared to be slaughtered, Swift demonstrates that a trend had appeared in politics to overlook the humanity of the nation's poor. Through his proposition that the children born of parents who cannot afford to support them should be murdered, Swift emphasises the way that the British are effectively killing the Irish people through their oppression and the extreme poverty they are inducing through their own greed.

HUMANS AS COMMODITIES

Swift's essay demonstrates that the English seem to treat the Irish people as little more than objects which contribute to the Irish economy. In appearing to make the serious argument that infants should be slaughtered for the tables of the wealthy, Swift is drawing attention to the fact that the humanity of even the youngest of the Irish population has been stripped away through the greed and oppression of the English ruling class. Through his reference to the poor of Ireland as statistics and numbers in calculations, Swift asks the reader to recognise that this is all the poor have become to the rich aristocracy who are predominantly concerned with preserving and increasing their means. The full title of the text makes clear that the purpose of the proposal is to prevent the poor from being a burden on the country, and an economic one at that.

Swift's arguments liken the children that he suggests be reared for the landlord's table to the pigs that are bred for the same purpose. In his calculations on how many infants to keep for breeding and how many to sell, he says that one male to four females is the ratio used for animals and that will therefore also suffice for the purpose he has at hand. Further, Swift raises the issue of whether children between the ages of 12 and 14 could be used to supplement the venison meat that has been diminished. His rejection of this proposal is based on a comparison of the toughness and taste of the two different types of meat, as he concludes that the flesh of a teenage boy in particular would be too tough. He does refer to the cruelty of such a measure, but seemingly as an afterthought, and even then only seems to be concerned with how it might be perceived.

POVERTY AND MOTHERHOOD

In the opening paragraph of *A Modest Proposal*, Swift gives a description of the poor mother and her children that can be witnessed begging on the Irish streets. For the duration of the essay, the emphasis stays on the poverty-stricken mothers and their children. Swift outlines how Irish mothers are the most disadvantaged in Irish society (a very forward-thinking feminist perspective for the time he was writing in). He demonstrates how their ability to work is inhibited by their role as carer for the children they bear, and this in turn worsens their state of poverty. It is this observation that forms the basis of Swift's proposal.

Swift goes on to represent the Irish mother as emotionally detached from her offspring as he moves further into his proposal. He suggests that poor mothers who would earn money from the sale of their babies would gladly do this, and without any hesitation. This is another satirical tool, as upper-class mothers would obviously be shocked at the suggestion and therefore be forced to recognise that the maternal feelings of Irish mothers of the lower class are no different to their own.

FURTHER REFLECTION

- Do you think Swift's use of satire was an effective way of capturing the attention of his audience at the time of publication and forcing them to think about the state of their society? Why/why not?
- Swift's text is almost three centuries old. Do you think it still has a relevant message today? If so, what is that message and why is it still important in the present day?
- Compare this text to another piece of Swift's writing of a different type (e.g. poetry or fiction). Are there similarities in his writing style between these texts? If so, what are they?
- Comment on the choice of title for this text. Do you like it? Why/why not? Would you have chosen an alternative title?
- Do you think an awareness of the historical context of *A Modest Proposal* is crucial in understanding and appreciating the text?
- Highlight some examples of satire in the text.

- When you read the text, were you more shocked or amused by the content and style of delivery? What do you think the more common reader reaction would have been at the time the essay was published?
- Can you think of any examples of satirical writing that you would come across in the present day?

We want to hear from you!
Leave a comment on your online library
and share your favourite books on social media!

FURTHER READING

REFERENCE EDITION

- Swift, J. (1996) *A Modest Proposal and Other Satirical Works.* New York: Dover Publications Inc.

MORE FROM BRIGHTSUMMARIES.COM

- Reading guide – *Gulliver's Travels* by Jonathan Swift.

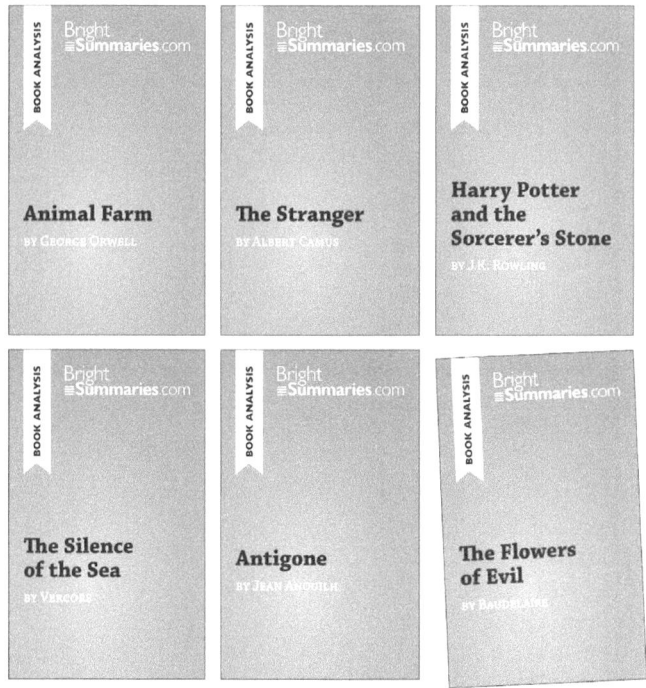

Although the editor makes every effort to verify the accuracy of the information published, BrightSummaries.com accepts no responsibility for the content of this book.

www.brightsummaries.com

Ebook EAN: 9782808018951

Paperback EAN: 9782808018968

Legal Deposit: D/2019/12603/114

Cover: © Primento

Digital conception by Primento, the digital partner of publishers.